UNDERSTANDING

The Epistle to the Hebrews

**BIBLE STUDIES
THROUGH THE BOOK
VERSE BY VERSE, CHAPTER BY CHAPTER**

lyngitchel@gmail.com

© Copyright March 2014 by Lyn Gitchel.

Note: This booklet is copyrighted to prevent changes and misuse, but it may be quoted from in whole, or in part, without further permission, providing due acknowledgement is given.

ISBN: 978-1497559004

Except where indicated, all scripture quotations are from the King James' Version of the Bible.

Occasionally quotations from *The Living Bible* or *The Message* are used.

The Living Bible, Paraphrased. © by Tyndale House Publishers, Wheaton Illinois.

The Message: the Bible in contemporary language by Eugene H. Petersen. © 1993,1994, 1995 1996, 2000, 2001, 2002. used by permission of NavPress Publishing Group.

• CONTENTS •

SECTION 1 — INTRODUCING THE SON
Hebrews 1:1 to 4:13

The Son   Hebrews 1:1-3 7
Better than Angels   Hebrews 1:4-14 8
God's Purpose for Mankind   Hebrews 2:1-11 9
Common Origin   Hebrews 2:9-18 10
Partners of Christ   Hebrews 3:1-19 11
Rest vs. Unbelief   Hebrews 4:1-13 12

SECTION 2 — THE NEW HIGH PRIEST
Hebrews 4:14 to 8:5

Our Great High Priest   Hebrews 4:14 to 5:10 15
Foundations   Hebrews 5:11 to 6:18 16
Melchisedek   Hebrews 6:19 to 7:10 17
The Difference   Hebrews 7:11 to 8:5 18

SECTION 3 — THE NEW SACRIFICE
Hebrews 8:6 TO 10:20

The New Covenant   Hebrews 8:6 to 8:13 21
The New Atonement   Hebrews 9:1-15 22
Re-Appearing   Hebrews 9:16-28 23
Proof Offered   Hebrews 10:1-18 24
Through the Veil   Hebrews 10:19-20 25

SECTION 4 — THE NEW FAITH
Hebrews 10:21 TO 11:40

Cultivating Faith   Hebrews 10:21-39 29
Now Faith   Hebrews 11:1-6 30
Faith Defined - Noah   Hebrews 11:7 31
Faith Defined - Abraham   Hebrews 11:8-9 32
Faith Defined - Abraham   Hebrews 11:10 33
Faith Defined - Sarah   Hebrews 11:11 34
Faith Defined - Isaac   Hebrews 11:17-19 35
Faith Defined - Moses   Hebrews 11:24-26 36
Faith Defined - Passover   Hebrews 11:28 37
Faith Defined - Red Sea   Hebrews 11:29 38
Faith Defined - Jericho   Hebrews 11:30 39
Faith Defined - Rahab   Hebrews 11:31 40
Faith Defined - Jephthah   Hebrews 11:32-40 41

CONCLUSION — THE GOAL
Hebrews 12 and 13

The Pattern   Hebrews 12:1-13 44
Specific Instructions   Hebrews 12:14 to 13:25 45

Introduction...

It was my own search that led to this book. I found the Book of Hebrews hard to understand and so — I say it to my shame — I avoided it. Finally I had enough sense to ask the Holy Spirit to open it up to me.

It took a lot more prayer and thought than some of the other epistles had, but I was amazed as understanding came step by step and verse by verse.

Walk with me through these pages, always remembering one fundamental truth that God showed to me: the book was not written to Gentile believers such as most of us are, but to Jewish people. These were people who had a foundation knowledge of the Old Testament and who based their lives and their religion upon it. Thus the writer reasons from the Old Testament and it is essential that we see it from that point of view also. To try and interpret Hebrews in the same way as most other epistles only causes confusion.

It will become clear as we go step by step. Go with me now and see Jesus from a Jewish concept.

—Lyn Gitchel
March 2014

UNDERSTANDING
The Epistle to the Hebrews

SECTION ONE
INTRODUCING THE SON
Hebrews 1:1 to 4:13

• SECTION ONE •
THE SON

Hebrews 1:1-3

"Who being the brightness of his glory, and the express image of his person."

First of all we need to see this: it's all about the Son. The Hebrews had never known the concept that God, the one true God, could have a Son. They had always had the prophets to help them understand God, but now, the writer explains, they have a greater revelation of God: a Son.

This Son, the writer explains, is the "express image" of God Himself. The words mean an "exact representation," as if it were a photo copy, only in person.

And that word translated "person" is interesting, too. It is the Greek word "hupostasis" and literally means: "understanding." Now, consider this: your understanding is how you think about a thing, how you perceive it. It's very personal, it's how your mind works. That's the key here. The Son's mind was stamped with the same mode of working as the mind of God. They thought alike because God made Him that way.

In fact, this Son revealed just who God is, the writer explains. The word translated "glory" is a word that actually means "reputation" and, if you think about it, a person's reputation is who they really are. Their character, their personality, their true nature. This is exactly what this word implies: that the Son was the true nature of God revealing exactly who God is and what He is like.

In other words, Jesus is who God is — exactly. And having made that statement, the writer goes on to say that this Son "by Himself purged our sins." That's an amazing thing, too, when you think about it because, having stated that this Son is the exact representation of God, the One who thinks like Him and totally acts like Him, the writer now goes on to say that this God-representation person was the One who went to the lengths of dying for the sin of mankind. Formerly these Hebrew people relied on slaughtered animals offered on the altar of sacrifice to do that — now, God has sent His own representative to do that very same thing.

• TWO •
BETTER THAN ANGELS

Hebrews 1:4-14

"Being made so much better than the angels..."

It is necessary for us to recognize that angels in the Bible are not beings with wings made of feathers who wear long flowing garments, and are mostly pictured as female. Our own tradition has made them that way.

In the Bible, angels that are involved with humans take on the form of a human being. Check out Genesis 18 and 19 where angels appeared to Abraham and to Lot. They appeared as men. Check out Joshua 5:13-15 where an angel appeared to Joshua, and Judges 13:3-6 where an angel appeared to Manoah's wife. In the New Testament, in Acts 12:10-11, see how Peter didn't realize it was an angel who delivered him from prison until the angel vanished. Then Peter said, "Now know I of a surety that the Lord hath sent his angel..." That angel might have been dressed as a prison guard in order to have Peter obey and follow him.

In the Bible, angels assume the form and garments appropriate for the visit they are making. Angels that have been seen today do just the same. It is true that there are Cherubim and Seraphim that have wings and are glorious in appearance, but these are different from the ministering angels that appear on earth.

Hebrew people would have understood this and, to them, it might have been easy to assume Jesus was just another angel, sent with a message and to minister to those who needed help. The writer shows that this is not the case and gives several reasons why Jesus was not an angel:

v.4. Angels are not, by inheritance, in the family of God.

v.5. Angels are not begotten of God, do not have a father/son relationship with God.

v.6. Angels are not to be worshipped.

v.7-8. Angels are not intended to be rulers.

v.10. Angels did not create the earth and the heavens.

v.12. God has never asked an angel to sit at His right hand. They are simply ministering spirits sent, the writer explains, to help bring people to the knowledge of salvation, the salvation that Jesus paid for by His death.

• THREE •
GOD'S PURPOSE FOR MANKIND

Hebrews 2:1-11

"How shall we escape, if we neglect so great salvation; which at the first began to be spoken by the Lord, and was confirmed unto us by them that heard him."

Having established the fact that Jesus was not an angel messenger but someone greater than that, the writer goes on to say that we therefore need to listen especially closely to what this Man taught.

He follows with a short teaching on the origin of man, God's original intention and what now lies in the future.

Vs. 6-7 talk about man, how he was created to be "a little lower than the angels" and set in this world to be in control of the earth. While everything, including the animal creation, was made subject to him, mankind was to remain subject to God and to remain strictly under His command.

It was when Adam and Eve decided to do things their own way and make their own choices that this system got messed up and evil entered the world.

That mankind should be in charge of the created world was God's original intention, This is mentioned in v. 8. "But now we see not all things put under him" refers, not to Jesus reigning in glory, but to present-day mankind—us. "When God put them in charge of everything, nothing was excluded. But we don't see it yet, don't see everything under human jurisdiction," is how *The Message* translates vs. 8.

Vs. 9-11 show how Jesus became one of us in order to right the whole messed-up plan. It could not be set right any other way. Mankind had given the world into the hands of evil and only one of the same mankind could redeem the situation and set it right.

He, who "for whom are all things, and by whom are all things," lowered Himself to become one of us in order to take on Himself the penalty of the world's evil. Then, dying for that sin, He overcame and now is able to raise those that believe, not just into salvation, the state of forgiveness for their own sin, but to the original intention for man. It was always God's intention for mankind to be a ruling people and to rule and reign is His plan for redeemed believers.

• FOUR •
COMMON ORIGIN

Hebrews 2:9-18

"For both he that sanctifieth and they who are sanctified are all of one: for which cause he is not ashamed to call them brethren."

It had to be done this way! God had made humankind and put them in charge of this world. Because God didn't want puppets but obedient and willing servants, He also gave them freewill. By making their own choices, the couple messed up the whole program and passed it on to all of their descendants—us. Some call that passing on "original sin."

So in order to right the problem, God created another human being, Jesus. Jesus was, as Adam was, fully human with the divine nature (mind) within Him. He also had freewill and could make His own choices. But Jesus, chose to do it the God-way. In all things He obeyed.

In vs. 10, it says "For it became him, for whom are all things, and by whom are all things, in bringing many sons unto glory, to make the captain of their salvation perfect through sufferings." The word "captain" in the Greek original is *archagos* and means author or originator. In other words Jesus laid the foundation for the situation to change.

"Perfect through sufferings" is also interesting. The word "perfect" is the Greek word *teleioo* and means the desired end was completed or accomplished. And "sufferings" does not necessarily indicate pain suffering. The word, which is *pathema,* means experiences, hardships undergone.

At the end of the passage for this study, it indicates that because "he himself hath suffered being tempted, he is able to succour them that are tempted," and Hebrews 4:15 says Jesus "was in all points tempted like as we are, yet without sin." When you think about it, this is awesome! In order to be able to show His followers how to deal with all the happenings in life, Jesus had to experience each thing Himself. His teaching is full of how to deal with situations and how to avoid being snared by temptation when faced by it. To know that Jesus' also had to deal with any problem you or I might experience is reassuring to say the least. He understands because He's been there!

• FIVE •
PARTNERS OF CHRIST

Hebrews 3:1-19

"For we are made partakers of Christ, if we hold the beginning of our confidence stedfast unto the end."

This is a difficult chapter to understand so let's take it a little at a time. First of all let's look at the first few verses which mention Moses. Remember, this was written to Jewish people to whom Moses was an extremely important person. The mention of him here is an endeavor to prove that Jesus was greater and more important than Moses.

The word "house" comes again and again and we need to remember that some of the words used in the King James' Version have changed their meaning slightly over the years. Here, the word translated "house" in the original Greek does not imply a residence. It is a dwelling, not to live in but to build in the same way as a calling or job assignment is given.

In this case, the assignment God gave to Moses was to construct a place of worship, a special tent that was to be used in the wilderness travels. And in that assignment, long before there were any written scriptures, God painted a picture of Jesus and the redemption that was to be achieved through Him.* That's what "a testimony of things which were to be spoken after" means.

While Moses was faithful in his God-given assignment, Jesus had a different assignment, a God-given assignment that involves us, the writer explains.

In the verses that follow, the writer exhorts his readers to see this and not to turn away through unbelief. Just as Moses delivered the people from the bondage of Egypt and brought them to the edge of the Promised Land but they then refused to enter because of fear and unbelief, readers are urged to see that Jesus also came to deliver from bondage, the slavery of sin, but they too could fail to enter into the fulfillment of the promise of His coming by similar fear and unbelief.

Those that enter by faith become "partakers of Christ" — the word means partners, associates, used in the same sense as partners share in the benefits of a corporate body.

*This is the subject of a different study, *Jesus in the Tabernacle, God's Blueprint for Redemption,* which is available separately.

• SIX •
REST vs. UNBELIEF

Hebrews 4:1-13

"He that is entered into his rest, he also hath ceased from his own works..."

Again we have to take into consideration that this was written to the Jewish people who were relying upon keeping of the law to be their salvation.

Not long ago I heard an old lady say, "I live in fear that I might do something or say something that will cause me to lose my salvation." I felt sad that she had been taught this way and that she was unable to rely completely on the sacrifice of Jesus to be her salvation.

While some churches teach that you can lose salvation, others teach you cannot. This is not the place to enter into that discussion but simply to endorse what the writer here was saying to Jewish people, who also felt they had to work hard to keep the law in order to merit eternal life.

With the whole emphasis of the book on Jesus and what He accomplished, the writer is saying that it is time to trust that the work of salvation is done, completed. It isn't something we have to do for ourselves but something we have to trust that it is already done by Jesus.

Resting is, in many ways, the same as trusting. I once asked God to explain this to me and He directed my thoughts toward being in bed. I realized that when you lie in bed you don't have one foot hanging over to the floor in case the bed gives way under you. You trust the bed to hold you. You rest in the fact it has been made to carry your weight.

The reference to God resting on the seventh day is interesting. In the original Greek, the word used for rest in v.4 is not quite the same as the others used here. Used of God, the word means that He stopped creating because the work was finished. It was completed so He rested. The same is true of our salvation. Jesus did all that was necessary; it is completed. All we need to do is rest in that fact, trust in His sacrifice to be enough. It is true there is a need to stay faithful to Him and to keep on keeping on in the spiritual walk, but, as the last verse in this passage points out, God knows all about our weaknesses.

UNDERSTANDING

The Epistle to the Hebrews

SECTION TWO
THE NEW HIGH PRIEST
HEBREWS 4:14 TO 8:5

We need to understand...

...that the writer to the Hebrews is addressing Jewish people and in the first section he has simply introduced Jesus.

The Hebrew people never had considered God might have a Son. The One God — the One and only — had been the center of their religious beliefs all through the Old Testament.

So the idea had to be introduced to them and the writer shows how it was necessary for God to achieve the original purpose for the world through another human person. But this human person could not inherit the sin-nature that had been passed down to all humanity from the original couple, he had to be human, but something different.

Now having introduced the Son and spoken briefly about what He achieved and the necessity for transferring their faith from law-keeping to Jesus, the writer goes on to explain the ministry of Jesus using the Old Testament symbols that God had set there to point forward to Jesus.

• SEVEN •
OUR GREAT HIGH PRIEST

Hebrews 4:14 to 5:10

"Seeing then that we have a great high priest, that is passed into the heavens, Jesus the Son of God, let us hold fast our profession." —v.14

"...after the order of Melchisedek." — v.10

The writer of the epistle, though we are not sure who he is, is certainly a Jewish person himself. He knew the Old Testament and constantly refers to it as a basis for what he is saying. Here it is no different.

Melchisedek comes on the scene in Genesis 14. Abram had just won a tremendous victory and was returning after the battle. With only 318 servants, he and his followers had conquered the armies of four kings and taken the loot and captives, among whom was his own nephew, Lot, and his family.

The four kings had previously invaded the area and subdued it. They were the conquerors — until Abram took it back from them. Technically, as conqueror, he then owned all the territory taken back, which included the territories of five local kings. Maybe Abram thought this was the first round won in the possession of the land God had promised him.

But Melchisedek, king of Salem, intercepted him and spent some time talking with him. Think about this: Abram, called by God out of a pagan environment, had walked alone in his faith with the God he had discovered. This king, the Bible says, was a priest of that same true God. Imagine the fellowship they would have had and the talk-time that must have followed. We also know that after a little time with Melchisedek, Abram knew whose the victory really was and said, "I have lifted up mine hand unto the Lord, the most high God, the possessor of heaven and earth, that I will not take from a thread even to a shoe latchet.."

The key to this passage lies in the fact that Melchisedek was there when Abram needed him, there to guide him and make sure he did not move outside of the intended faith-walk God had for him. "After the order of Melchisedek," as describing Jesus our own high priest indicates that, since He has walked the road of humanity, He is able to do the same for us. And that's what this passage says.

• EIGHT •
FOUNDATIONS

Hebrews 5:11 to 6:18

"...ye have need that one teach you again which be the first principles of the oracles of God..."

At first sight, it seems as if the writer is chastising his readers for being childish in their spiritual walk, but after praying about it and thinking about it, I don't think that this is the emphasis intended.

When God delivered the Israelites from Egypt with the help of Moses, He didn't intend that they camp right outside the gates of Egypt. God intended that they go on going on until they reached the Promised Land.

Similarly, in our Christian walk, God does not intend that we camp just outside receiving salvation and go no further in our spiritual growth. He wants us to move on into all that is there for us.

Here, the writer seems to be encouraging the Jewish readers to move on from what they have always held so dear and to realize that all of it is just a foundation for what Jesus has achieved.

Actually the whole Book of Hebrews is about this same thing: that the Old Testament religious rituals were looking forward to something greater, and that greater something is found in Jesus.

At the beginning of Chapter 6, the writer speaks of "not laying again the foundation of repentance from dead works" and, as we try and see this from a Jewish point of view, we need to remember that they had been raised to the belief that keeping the law — works — was the way of salvation. They also had extensive cleansing rites of immersion in a *mikveh* which had to be followed before attending worship services and this may be what is referred to by "baptisms." The word simply means "immersions."

They also believed in laying hands on their sacrifices before the animal was killed and offered for the forgiveness of sin — but we'll see more of that in later chapters.

For now it's enough the realize that all the Old Testament pointed toward Jesus. Jesus was God's Promise, and, as the writer points out, since God cannot fail, the Promise is here so it's time to leave the former things and move forward.

• NINE •
MELCHISEDEK

Hebrews 6:19 to 7:10

"...Jesus, made an high priest for ever after the order of Melchisedec. Melchisedec, king of Salem, priest of the most high God...first being by interpretation King of righteousness, and after that also King of Salem, which is, King of peace."

While it is a mystery who this Melchisedek actually was, here we need only see his qualifications for being likened to the Son of God and for Jesus having been identified with his particular ministry.

The most important qualification offered is that he was "priest of the most high God." In days and locations where heathen worship was the norm, this is amazing. No evidence of scholarly training or of legal inheritance is offered. Rather it is to the contrary; these two facts are denied. He is simply a representative of the One True God.

Second is an interpretation of his name, Melchisedek. The two words *melchi,* which means king, and *sedek* which means righteousness, further tell us about him. He is a representative of righteousness, the true righteousness of the one true God. The right way of doing things.

The old city of Salem later became the central point of the Jewish and Christian faiths: Jerusalem. But here it is simply the name that is in emphasis. *Salem* means peace. So Melchisedek also represented peace, God's peace. God's method of doing things in His time and in His way.

When King Melchisedek went to meet Abraham as he was returning after winning back the territory from four kings, Abraham was victorious. He was now the rightful owner of the territory. But after meeting with Melchisedek he stated that he would not take "even a shoe latchet." Melchisedek was sent to show Abraham that God had it in all in control His way. There was a right way, a peaceful way for the promise God had given Abraham to be fulfilled. Fighting to achieve God promises is not God's way.

This passage, showing that Jesus has the same ministry to us, is a the lesson that God has His right way, His time and His peaceful way for bringing about His promises in our lives. We do not have to fight for them; just to rest in the promise and know He will bring it about in His own way.

• TEN •
THE DIFFERENCE

Hebrews 7:11 to 8:5

"If therefore perfection were by the Levitical priesthood, (for under it the people received the law,) what further need was there that another priest should rise after the order of Melchisedec, and not be called after the order of Aaron?"

A Jewish person might argue here that since salvation was made possible by keeping the law, and since absolution was made possible by the sacrificial system, why was there need for a different kind of high priest?

So this passage explains that the Levitical priests were indeed ordained to offer sacrifices which at the time cleansed the offerer of sin, but a long-term solution was not offered. While the Levitical priests ministered by offering sacrifices to cleanse from a particular wrongdoing they were unable to offer any solution that would avoid doing the same thing again. It was indeed a temporary solution.

We have already seen how King Melchisedek, priest of the Most High God, ministered guidance and fellowship to Abraham at a time when he needed it. When He is called a high priest like Melchisedek, it indicates that Jesus is able to go that extra mile in helping us. He is able to offer help with our spiritual walk, help in overcoming temptation and guidance as to the right way to handle things. The scriptures say that He was "not an high priest which cannot be touched with the feeling of our infirmities; but was in all points tempted like as we are, yet without sin" and "in that he himself hath suffered being tempted, he is able to succour them that are tempted" "seeing he ever liveth to make intercession for them." (Heb. 4:15; 2:18; 7:25.)

The difference is clear: priests of the Levitical order were able to take care of past wrongdoing by a sacrifice, but Jesus as our high priest is able to have a personal relationship with each believer, helping him or her through difficulties and guiding as to the right way of dealing with problems.

The word intercession in the Greek actually means *to reason with*. While the intercessor is a "go-between," it indicates a counseling session, like talking a thing over — and that was exactly the ministry of King Melchisedek. And of Jesus, too.

UNDERSTANDING
The Epistle to the Hebrews

SECTION THREE
THE NEW SACRIFICE
HEBREWS 8:6 TO 10:20

We need to understand...

...that as the writer to the Hebrews addresses Jewish people, he is moving slowly as he introduces Jesus.

This is a whole new concept for them to grasp, something very different from measuring up by keeping laws and obeying commandments.

In addition, remember that it had been this way for thousands of years and so to introduce so drastic a change as a life by faith instead of works was dramatic. They needed to be given time to reason this out.

All the way through the Book of Hebrews, the writer constantly refers to the Old Testament customs and rites of worship, showing how they were all pointing to the One who was to come, and that this One was Jesus.

The case for Jesus, that the writer has to make to the Jewish people, is that the old ways were not working, sin did not go away by efforts to live a good life. Something greater was required to bring about fellowship between God and mankind.

• ELEVEN •
THE NEW COVENANT

Hebrews 8:6 to 8:13

"For this is the covenant that I will make with the house of Israel after those days, saith the Lord; I will put my laws into their mind, and write them in their hearts: and I will be to them a God, and they shall be to me a people."

Covenant — an agreement between God and mankind — is spoken of a number of times in the scripture but here only two are mentioned. The first is found in the Old Testament as given to Moses: *"And Moses went up unto God, and the Lord called unto him out of the mountain, saying, Thus shalt thou say to the house of Jacob, and tell the children of Israel; Ye have seen what I did unto the Egyptians, and how I bare you on eagles' wings, and brought you unto myself. Now therefore, if ye will obey my voice indeed, and keep my covenant, then ye shall be a peculiar treasure unto me above all people: for all the earth is mine: And ye shall be unto me a kingdom of priests, and an holy nation. These are the words which thou shalt speak unto the children of Israel. And Moses came and called for the elders of the people, and laid before their faces all these words which the Lord commanded him. And all the people answered together, and said, All that the Lord hath spoken we will do. And Moses returned the words of the people unto the Lord."* (Exodus 19:3-8.) This one is based upon the condition "if ye will obey... and keep..."

The one spoken of in writing to the Hebrews is different. In this one, quoted from Jeremiah 31:31-34, God says "I will put my laws in their mind, and write them on their hearts." God is speaking about the birth of a new nature, a divine Spirit-birthed nature, within the lives of the redeemed.

While the old covenant required that they measure up and keep God's laws, it was found throughout history that this was not possible. People were so born into sinful ways that they could not get themselves out of the rut.

So God sent Jesus. Jesus, born by the action of the Holy Spirit on the body of Mary, was not born with the original sin nature inherited by all humans since Adam. He was not subject to the sin-penalty that had fallen on all mankind. When Jesus died it was voluntarily, a sacrifice to bring the world back into line with the mind of God.

• TWELVE •
THE NEW ATONEMENT

Hebrews 9:1-15

"... by his own blood he entered in once into the holy place, having obtained eternal redemption for us."

Jewish readers understood about the Day of Atonement. Leviticus 16 explains how God ordered that only the high priest could enter the Holy of Holies, and only once a year. The Day of Atonement took place on the 10th of the seventh month and was a very special time of fasting and prayer for the Jewish people. And it was the only time the high priest entered the Holy of Holies, the only time anyone was allowed into the direct presence of God.

This is what is referred to here in this passage in Hebrews. The writer makes it clear that the "way into the holiest of all was not yet made manifest, while as the first tabernacle was yet standing," it pointed forward in symbolic picture-form to what Jesus would later achieve. (Heb. 9:8.)

"But Christ being come an high priest of good things to come...by his own blood he entered in once into the holy place, having obtained eternal redemption for us." (vs. 11-12.)

There is more to see about this entering in, but for now let's just stop and look at how amazing this is and the immensity of the sacrifice Jesus made for us. We tend to see only the suffering He went through, and while this is enormous, and incredible that He would be willing to suffer that much for us, there is something more to consider.

Jesus is the only human being who led such a perfect, sinless life. Remember, sin is simply moving out of the direct will of God. We saw how Adam and Eve were put in charge of everything with only one restriction: that they lived under the direct supervision of God. They moved out of this by one simple choice and brought sin to the rest of mankind. Jesus never moved out of the direct will of God. He is the only person who ever earned the right to walk straight into heaven on his own merit. But He gave it away. He took our sin and lost the right to enter heaven. Hebrews 9:12 tells us that He entered the presence of God "by His own blood." How amazing is that! He belonged there but couldn't enter. He entered as a sinner like the rest of us, on the merit of the blood of His own sacrifice.

• THIRTEEN •
RE-APPEARING

Hebrews 9:16-28

"For Christ is not entered into the holy places made with hands, which are the figures of the true; but into heaven itself, now to appear in the presence of God for us."

It has been said that when the high priest entered into the Holy of Holies on the Day of Atonement, they tied a rope around him so that, if he died, they could haul him out. I have heard several preachers say this but personally I cannot find any mention of it in the scriptures.

The high priest had a unique set of garments that were God-ordained for him to wear when ministering. One of these, a robe of blue, worn under the *ephod* which carried the breastplate. Around the bottom of it were little round things like pomegranates alternating with little bells. The bells were not the same as those we see today but were hit from the outside, like a gong. It would seem the little pomegranates might be the clappers for these bells.

The reason for such a strange hem surrounding this garment is given in Exodus 28:34-35. The bells were to tinkle all the time the high priest moved around in the sanctuary so that the people knew that he was still alive.

And why was it so important that he was still alive? So that the people knew that the sacrifice had been accepted and their sin purged. He hadn't been struck dead.

This also is one of the greatest reasons for Jesus' resurrection. The sacrifice has been accepted; death has been conquered. When Jesus rose again, He rose as the Savior of the world.

Jesus took the blood of His own sacrifice into the Holy of Holies, into the presence of God Himself, and offered it for the salvation of sin-torn mankind. When they laid their hands on the animal sacrifices in the Old Testament the sin of the person was by faith transferred to the animal; when the animal was killed the sin was atoned for. So, in the same way, the scriptures tell us that God laid on Jesus the sin of mankind (Isaiah 53:6), and when He died the sin penalty was paid. Then He entered the presence of God, presented the blood of His own sacrifice. When He rose again, the victorious Savior, the sacrifice had been accepted.

• FOURTEEN •
PROOF OFFERED

Hebrews 10:1-18

"For the law having a shadow of good things to come, and not the very image of the things, can never with those sacrifices which they offered year by year continually make the comers thereunto perfect. For then would they not have ceased to be offered? because that the worshippers once purged should have had no more conscience of sins. But in those sacrifices there is a remembrance again made of sins every year."

The argument offered here is clear. If the law had done the job of making mankind perfect, sacrifices could then have been discontinued. The fact that they had to go on meant that the law did not finalize the work.

And then the writer goes on to point out that God had no pleasure in sacrifices. Heathen gods were offered sacrifices because the followers thought the gods were pleased by them. But, for the Jewish people in Old Testament times, the sacrifices had been for one reason only, to make atonement for their sin, or in other words to pay the price of it. It wasn't that God liked sacrifice; it was that sin made it necessary.

By sending Jesus, God cut out the need for continual sacrifice and took care of the problem once and for all. He refers back to Heb. 8:10 where he had quoted the new covenant that God was ushering in, the covenant that would write the laws of God in their minds and hearts. In effect it was the introduction of a new nature to be born into people.

Then the writer goes on to show that the sacrifice of Jesus — the once-for-all sacrifice that He had voluntarily submitted to — was the method by which God birthed this new nature into the hearts of believing and willing followers. And Jesus is now seated at the right hand of God to authorize the process. "From henceforth expecting..." indicates this. The word *expecting* is the Greek work *ekdechomai* and is made up of two Greek words *ek* indicating the direction from which a thing comes, and *dechomai* indicating acceptance of the responsibility. He is in charge of salvation now, it has changed from the old to the new covenant and "there is no more offering for sin" because it has all been taken care of. Our relationship with God is now all in the hands of Jesus.

• FIFTEEN •
THROUGH THE VEIL

Hebrews 10:19-20

"Having therefore, brethren, boldness to enter into the holiest by the blood of Jesus, By a new and living way, which he hath consecrated for us, through the veil, that is to say, his flesh."

If you look back at the story in Mark 15:37-38, the account of the tearing of the temple veil at the time when Jesus died now takes on new meaning. It is especially significant since it was torn from the top to the bottom, indicating that it had to be something that God carried out. Man would only have been able to tear it from the bottom upward since the height of the Holy of Holies inside the temple was 20 cubits which is about 30 ft. (1 Kings 6:20.) And probably, if man had been able to tear the massive veil at all, it would have torn very little or would have taken a lot of strong men to tear it at all.

But God did it.

Imagine the impact when, at the moment Jesus died, the skies went dark and there was a huge tearing sound as the massive veil was torn. It's hard to see how the religious leaders could have ignored so great a sign of the efficacy of Jesus' claim to be the Son of God, and it makes you wonder how they would have felt in that moment if they had considered that Jesus might have been who He said He was — and they had gone ahead and killed Him.

Surely, the tearing of the veil at that moment was one of the greatest signs ever to happen at that time.

But God made a point that went down in history: the way into the presence of God was now open to anyone who cared to believe and enter. No more was it a once-a-year entering in by one man only, the high priest, to offer the blood of a sacrifice for the sins of the people for that past year. The one-time sacrifice was now made, Jesus had lived the perfect life and chosen to die, by His death taking the penalty of mankind on Himself. By that one-time sacrifice He made, the way into the presence of God was now open to all.

So the writer challenged his readers to do just that, to enter the presence of God, trusting in the sacrifice of Jesus, and there to find strength and help to live the new life being offered.

So what have we learned so far?

We have learned that in addressing Jewish people, the writer had to move slowly. They had a God-ordained law of sacrifice for the removal of sin, and God-ordained rites and rituals that had been in effect for years.

In seeking to usher in a new era, along with a bunch of new ideas, he had to move slowly and carefully, pointing out that the old had been a foundation for the new. Each Old Testament rite and ritual had been there, not to a be a permanent fixture, but to point forward to Jesus.

The most important change was probably the hardest of all: that now they were no longer to rely upon working at their own salvation, but to receive it by simple, trusting faith.

UNDERSTANDING
The Epistle to the Hebrews

SECTION FOUR
THE NEW FAITH
HEBREWS 10:21 TO 11:40

FACTS ABOUT FAITH

Faith is required. (Hebrews 11:6)

Faith sometimes can change the circumstances.

Faith sometimes does not change the circumstances but works on changing the individual.

Faith does not judge God, but it is OK to address the problem with God and to complain about it.

Faith is content to let God work things out His way and in His time.

Faith always leads to victory.

• SIXTEEN •
CULTIVATING FAITH

Hebrews 10:21-39

"Let us hold fast the profession of our faith without wavering..."

Having moved on to the question of faith and that it replaces working at salvation through keeping the law, the writer now develops a study on faith itself. He addresses how to have it, how to keep it and what faith really is.

He gives suggestions on how to cultivate faith:

(1) Call to remembrance what God has done in the past and how He dealt with problems then. (Heb. 10:32.)

(2) Faith is developed like muscles are made strong, by use. Be ready, when there is a problem, to use faith and expect it to work on your behalf. (Heb. 10:22-24.)

(3) Associate with people who can help your faith grow. Don't try to find all the answers on your own. God made people to be a family and other believers can help. But be sure to associate with those who will build you up and strengthen your faith, not those who will pull you down. (Heb. 10:24-25.)

(4) Study the lives of great people of God who have used their faith. We shall do this as we study Chapter 11, but other biographies are available. The books that you read have great impact on your life so it is wise to choose carefully.

(5) Seek an understanding of faith, its characteristics, how it works and what is required of a believer. Seek to understand how to use faith, and also how not to become snared in over-zealous super-spirituality. Remember the story of the man who was trapped in a flood. He had gone onto his housetop to get away from the water and was crying out to God for help. Rescuers came by in a boat and offered to take him to safety, but he refused saying He was asking God to save him and make the waters go away. A while after that a helicopter hovered overhead and dropped a lifeline to the man but he refused it saying he was trusting God to save him. Needless to say, he stayed on the roof until the waters receded. God had sent the help needed but he had refused it.

(6) Ask God to strengthen your faith, but understand that faith is strengthened by using it, so the answer might come as problems you might have to face!

• SEVENTEEN •
NOW FAITH

Hebrews 11:1-6

"Now faith is the substance of things hoped for, the evidence of things not seen."

While I know that this is not the way the writer meant it, it is helpful to consider the word *now* as qualifying the word *faith*. For example, faith that is anchored in the present is far more likely to achieve results than faith that thinks in terms of someday it might happen!

Imagine that you have a lamp and an electrical outlet. It's dark in the room and you need light, You have the lamp and you know it will light if you plug it in the outlet. But you have to plug it in *now*. It will not give you light if you figure you will plug it in someday! So, using faith, you pick up the plug and plug it into the outlet. Light results.

This illustration parallels faith in God. The darkness is your problem, the lamp is the potential answer to the problem. God compares to the electrical outlet, and the lamp cord with the plug at the end is your faith. Faith plugged into God, now, in the present time, will bring results. Hoping for an answer in the future sometime will bring just that.

But we need to note that God is in control of how the answer comes and when. He has His ways of doing things and we need to accept that, but He does promise that faith will bring an answer. As soon as you plug in your faith, the answer will begin to happen; how fast you experience it is up to God.

Substance is an interesting word, too. In the Greek it is *hupostasis* and is made up of two root words.

The first part *hupo* means *the agent* or *the means* of doing a thing. The second word *stasis* comes from the root word that means *to stand* as in when you are building something and the framework is set up. It means *to establish*.

The Living Bible renders this verse like this: *What is faith? It is the confident assurance that something we want is going to happen. It is the certainty that what we hope for is waiting for us, even though we cannot see it up ahead."* There the word *substance* is rendered *confident assurance* and that really describes what faith is. After all, when you plug in that lamp you have the confident assurance the light will go on!

• EIGHTEEN •
FAITH DEFINED

Hebrews 11:7

"By faith Noah, being warned of God of things not seen as yet, moved with fear, prepared an ark to the saving of his house..."

Genesis 6:5 to 7:24

The story of Noah is so incredible. God commanded a man to build a huge box, 450 feet long. A football field is 360 feet so imagine how big it was! It was 75 feet wide and 45 feet high to include first, second and third 15ft-high floors. And, presumably, this was built before the days of power tools!

And what is more amazing is that God was asking this man to build a huge boat the size of an ocean liner when presumably there had never been any rain on the earth and Noah wouldn't know what rain or flooding was. We are told in Gen. 2:5-6 that the earth was watered by a mist and there were rivers, we know that, but no mention is made of rain until Noah and his family experienced it full force.

Faith is believing and obeying God even when circumstances do not support what God has said.

Assuming that Noah's three sons were grown and able to help, still they would have had to cut down the trees, shape the timbers, come up with nails, and put those timbers together so they would not leak and all to deal with something that they didn't know what it was!

Then there was another test of faith. After the huge boat was finished, God told Noah to gather the animals of each species, and bring them into the boat. How Noah would have been able to do this is a mystery except for the fact that God said the animals "shall come unto thee" (Gen. 6:20.) so we can know God had something to do with it.

But after they were all gathered into the boat, and after Noah and his family had also taken up residence there, nothing special happened for seven more days. God had shut them in (Gen. 7:16.) — a scary thing when the door shuts behind you and you find it locked! But then they had to wait. They must have wondered during that wait, discussed among themselves if anything was really going to happen. God had said it. They just had to wait and believe.

• NINETEEN •
FAITH DEFINED

Hebrews 11:8-9

"By faith Abraham, when he was called to go out into a place which he should after receive for an inheritance, obeyed; and he went out, not knowing whither he went."

Genesis 12:1-5

Archeologists tell us that Abram's home town, Ur of the Chaldees, was a city with brick-built, two-floor-or-more buildings, with commerce and industry, and good education. Abram would probably have been a business man, prosperous and owning property. Religious life was pagan and the God that we know was as yet unknown among them. We learn from Joshua 24:2 and 14-15, that Abram's family did worship the pagan gods though how Abram came to know the true God is not told to us except that Acts 7:2 says that God appeared to him while Abram still lived Ur of the Chaldees, spoke to him and impressed him to leave his home and country and go out into the unknown.

> **Faith is resting (dwelling) in the promise of God even when circumstances do not endorse it.**

Note that God did not tell him anything specific about where he was to go, nor did He tell him it would be a better life. All God said was to go "into a land which I will shew thee." Abram had to put his faith in a formerly unknown God who would shew him an unknown land, at some unknown time.

All God required of Abram was to walk with Him in faith, not even knowing where. It is an amazing thing that God could have broken though into a family that was worshipping pagan gods, impressed this man that He was really the only true God, and have influenced him enough to make Abram willing to leave his home, his apparent prosperity and all that he knew of comfort, to travel to an unknown destiny somewhere.

Then, when he did arrive at the apparent destination, he dwelt in that land as a stranger, living in a tent, wandering as a nomad, seemingly belonging nowhere and having nothing but a promise to rest on. He simply had to trust the God who had spoken to him.

• TWENTY •
FAITH DEFINED

Hebrews 11:10
"For he looked for a city which hath foundations, whose builder and maker is God."

Genesis 12:4-8

Abraham was a remarkable man. First of all, he had left his home and country, left what was probably a comfortable life in a storied house and a prosperous lifestyle, to follow an unknown God to an unknown place. His goal became to go where God had told him to go — wherever that turned out to be.

When he finally did come into the land of Canaan, God spoke to him and said, "Unto thy seed will I give this land." Interesting, because both he and his wife were long past the child-bearing stage of life and he had no "seed" to inherit the promise God was giving.

Faith is believing God is doing what He said He would do

But notice what Abraham did: he "called on the name of the Lord."

To use an illustration here, a company that makes promises, like an insurance company for example, is only as good as the name of the company. Just anybody can't make those same promises. The name of the company is what is the assurance that stands behind the promises.

So we find that Abraham "called on the name of the Lord" continually. Everywhere he camped, it was the same. He built an altar and called on the name of the Lord. It was as if he was staking a claim, challenging God to make the promise come to pass.

We can learn from this today. It is easy to make a life for ourselves our own way. We do want God in our lives and we do want His blessing, but whether God is really the foundation of everything we do is the question. A life dedicated to and walking with God is not just a go-to-church-twice-a-week lifestyle and doing our own thing the rest of the time. It's a total commitment, finding His way of living, where He wants us to live, work, and how He wants us to raise a family. This kind of committed lifestyle is not a prison we put ourselves in! God does want us to be happy, fulfilled and to prosper in life, but He does want us to do it His way.

• TWENTY-ONE •
FAITH DEFINED

Hebrews 11:11

"Through faith also Sara herself received strength to conceive seed, and was delivered of a child when she was past age, because she judged him faithful who had promised."

Genesis 17:15-22

You have to look between the lines here to see what Sarah went through at this time. God had indicated that she would become pregnant and give birth to a son at ninety years old. Even if she could believe as far as the possibility that she could become pregnant at her age, there still was the added promise that it would yield a son. After all that's only a 50 percent chance!

Faith believes beyond the natural

But if you read on through the next chapters before the time that Sarah actually gave birth to Isaac, there are a couple of significant events there. And notice particularly that God set down a time frame and told Sarah that the birth of Isaac would occur "at this set time in the next year." (Gen. 17:21.)

First there is the account of the destruction of Sodom and Gomorrah. Imagine the after-effects of such a destruction — smoke and stench everywhere in the surrounding areas where the great cities had been. Abraham did not live far from there so it is not surprising that he packed up his tents and moved. Then in Chapter 20 we read the story of how Abraham pretended Sarah was not his wife and how she was taken into the harem of the king of that area. In the natural, that would have been a great honor for a man's sister; for Sarah it was near tragedy!

Can you imagine the despair that went through Sarah's thoughts as she sat day after day waiting for the dreaded time when the king would call for her. Presumably she was pregnant, or if not pregnant yet, she was resting on God's promise to her that she, as Abraham's wife, would bear him a son. And now this had happened!

In spite of very adverse circumstances, Sarah was called to believe that God would somehow keep His word and bring the promise to pass. That's faith!

• TWENTY-TWO •
FAITH DEFINED

Hebrews 11:17-19

"By faith Abraham, when he was tried, offered up Isaac: and he that had received the promises offered up his only begotten son..."

Genesis 22:1-18

It wasn't that Abraham didn't care about his son; he loved him a whole lot. The Bible emphasizes that in Genesis 22:1. And it wasn't that God didn't understand either because God explicitly said, "thy son, thine only son, Isaac, whom thou lovest." God knew, as well as Abraham did, that this lad was the one through whom He had promised to establish the covenant. And now God asks for him to be offered as a sacrifice? That's a hard, hard lesson, especially for Abraham. So why did God do this?

Faith is willing to risk believing the impossible

Abraham did not question God when God told him to take his beloved son and sacrifice him. He did not argue, he simply up and went. No arguing, no questions.

Abraham had such a complete trust in God that on the third day when they were about to arrive at the designated place, he was able to tell his servants "I and the lad will go yonder and will come again unto you."

When Isaac asked why they had no lamb for the burnt offering, Abraham again spoke in faith and said, "God will provide a lamb."

But the most wonderful thing of all was Abraham's willingness to give to God his only son whom he loved so dearly.

God had told Abraham that He was establishing a covenant with him and that is the key. Back in those days, when two tribal leaders made a covenant agreement between themselves, they made an exchange of property and sometimes even children. This happened especially between kings of countries that were making an agreement; a princess would be given to the king of the other country. Here God had found a man who was willing, and had the faith, to give his son to God. Abraham believed that God knew what He was doing and that somehow He would work it out. The act established a covenant exchange so that God could in turn give His son a sacrifice for mankind.

• TWENTY-THREE •
FAITH DEFINED

Hebrews 11:24-26

"By faith Moses, when he was come to years, refused to be called the son of Pharaoh's daughter, choosing rather to suffer affliction with the people of God..."

Exodus 3:1-12

It isn't easy to be called of God for a specific purpose. God never promised it would be. And most times the person does not feel adequate for the task. Moses, when God told him to go back to Egypt and lead the people out from slavery replied "Who am I, that I should go unto Pharaoh, and that I should bring forth the children of Israel out of Egypt?"

Faith is confident in the call of God in spite of the circumstances

And when Moses did undertake to follow the Lord's command, he was always being blamed for things that happened. The people blamed Moses and fussed at him after he had first approached Pharaoh and they had been given more slave-work to do in response. (Ex. 5:20-23.) And when Moses did lead out the 600,00 men, with their wives, children and the "mixed multitude" that went along and they ended up in front of the Red Sea, when they saw Pharaoh's armies they again blamed Moses for their predicament. (Ex. 14:11-12.)

Three days later, in front of an oasis where the water was not drinkable, Moses again took the blame, (Ex. 15:23-24.) and a month or so later, "Would to God we had died by the hand of the Lord in the land of Egypt, when we sat by the flesh pots, and when we did eat bread to the full; for ye have brought us forth into this wilderness, to kill this whole assembly with hunger," were the unkind words they shot at him. It was similar at Rephidim where there was also no water and when they reached Mount Sinai, God visibly manifested His presence on the mountain with thunder and lightning, speaking to Moses in front of them all, but they never did seem to get it. Is it any wonder that Moses complained to the Lord at one point that he was always having to bottle-feed these people. (Num. 11:11-12.)

But Moses remained firm in his resolve, discouraged at times, nevertheless true to the call God had placed on him.

• TWENTY-FOUR •
FAITH DEFINED

Hebrews 11:28
"Through faith he kept the passover, and the sprinkling of blood, lest he that destroyed the firstborn should touch them."
Exodus 12:1-23

We have to realize that, even when we can't see it, God has a reason for doing things the way He does them. It was important that the Hebrew people obey all the instructions for the Passover meal because God was painting a picture, a picture of Jesus.

They were not to question why the lamb had to be taken out of the flock and kept separate for three days before killing it on the fourth. When the lamb fussed at being caged up alone, they weren't to question why they couldn't leave it with the flock for those three days. They did not know it was a picture of the three and a half years of Jesus' ministry before He was killed as the Lamb of God to atone for the sin of the world.

Faith is obeying the instructions of God exactly word for word

They probably didn't question why the lamb had to be a perfect specimen, but they might have wanted to question why they couldn't save the leftovers for the next day. Why waste food?

And then again, why were they to dress in outdoor, traveling clothes when they ate this meal. Why not be comfortable while they ate and dress to leave afterward?

Painting the blood on the side posts and upper post of the entrance doors was a strange thing to do, but Moses did explain that this was to be a sign. But why the blood of the lamb? Why not just paint a sign on the door? They could not know it was to be a picture of the protecting blood of Jesus available to believers for centuries after.

Obeying God's instructions implicitly is so important. We have to get it right. Like back when God told Abraham to leave his country, his family and his father's house, Abraham took the family with him, it wasn't until after the death of his father and after God had worked a separation between Abraham and Lot that God was able to establish the covenant through him. Exact obedience is important.

• TWENTY-FIVE •
FAITH DEFINED

Hebrews 11:29

"By faith they passed through the Red sea as by dry land: which the Egyptians assaying to do were drowned."

Exodus 13:20 to 14:31

This third day in the Israelites' journey was destined to be a day of worship in the first place. When Moses received the command from God at the burning bush, God had said to him, "Thou shalt come...unto the king of Egypt, and ye shall say unto him, The Lord God of the Hebrews hath met with us: and now let us go, we beseech thee, three days' journey into the wilderness, that we may sacrifice to the Lord our God." (Exodus 3:18.) The idea of three days and then a time of worship was God's plan in the first place.

Faith walks through the problems when God opens the way

If you trace their route on a map, you will find that they were heading down the east side of the Red Sea on a well-known mining route. At Etham, God said "turn," and turned them right into the path of trouble. God knew the armies of Pharaoh would give chase and He turned them round so they would find themselves trapped between the Red Sea and the enemy. Yes! God did it!

Sometimes we also find ourselves caught between the devil and the deep blue sea! They couldn't go on because the sea was in front of them; they couldn't go back because the armies of Pharaoh had them cornered! Surely God must have made a mistake this time! But, no, God had a purpose that was beyond anything that they could see for themselves. He did not merely want them to come out from the slavery of Egypt and have their steps dogged by the armies of that country all the way through the wilderness. He wanted to destroy the power Egypt had over them for ever.

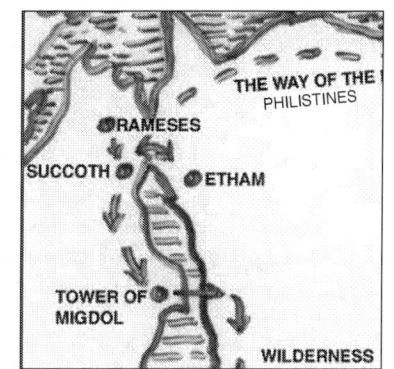

Finally they walked through the wall of trouble and it did turn out to be a day of worship after all, of great praise and thanksgiving.

• TWENTY-SIX •
FAITH DEFINED

Hebrews 11:30

"By faith the walls of Jericho fell down, after they were compassed about seven days."

Joshua 5:13 to 6:20

First, note that God said He had given them the city of Jericho. It is so important that we should line up with what God has in mind, not to try to line God up with what we have in mind. Sometimes, how God does a thing can seem to us to be strange, or even sometimes a little stupid. But God is well known for doing things in an out-of-the-ordinary way and this certainly was no exception.

It really might have seemed to them a little stupid. The city was about five miles to walk around and on the first six

Faith walks on in persistence until the problems fall away

days that would have been a chore, but no real difficulty. But on the seventh day, the day on which they were going to have to fight with the inhabitants face to face and fist to fist, God planned to tire them out before this even happened! A thirty five mile walk first and then a battle!!

It would not have worked if everyone had not cooperated with God's plan. If some had chosen not to show up one of the days, or had taken a break to go some place with the family, or if some had overslept or been too tired to walk that day, the plan would never have succeeded. It took full cooperation and everyone taking their place to be a part of the total effort and plan.

It's interesting here that the total triumph was due to two very "small" things — they walked around the city and they shouted at the precise moment God told them to. They didn't shout all the way round on the other six days, neither did they wrestle and cry in prayer, begging God for their victory. They just walked round the problem and then shouted in triumph at the moment they were told to.

And it was a joint thing, this project. Each person knew they had to play a part in it and that they need be concerned to do only as God had commanded. They were part of the unified whole, but each person needed to do his or her own part in that whole. Only then would the plan work.

• TWENTY-SEVEN •
FAITH DEFINED

Hebrews 11:31
"By faith the harlot Rahab perished not with them that believed not, when she had received the spies with peace."
Joshua 2 and 6:21-25

In those days, walls around the cities were huge, wide enough for a road to run around them on the top. This is where Rahab had her house, right on the wall.

Rahab had somehow found faith in the one true God. How we are not told, but her words to the spies show that she knew which God was the greater. "For the Lord your God, he is God in heaven above and in earth beneath," she said to them. And knowing that there would come a battle, she asked for protection in return for hiding the spies, which they agreed to.

Faith does not let fear control but trusts God instead

Only God knew what was going to happen to the walls of Jericho where her house stood, but Rahab had to have more faith than simply putting faith in the promise from the two spies. She was told to gather her family and take them all into her own house there on the wall. Maybe she faced arguments when she told them to come there, and what did they all think as they watched all those Israelites walk round the city day after day in silence and carrying that odd looking gold chest along with them. I think that would have created a really scary feeling, a fearful dread of what was about to happen.

But on the seventh day, when the shout came from the voices of hundreds of men who had been silent to that time, the walls began to shake beneath them and by faith they had to stay in that shaking house and not run out to escape as instinct would have dictated. I think that might be what called for the most faith, for Rahab to keep her family inside that house when it was shaking so violently and to keep them calm as they watched the walls fall away all around them. But stay they did for they were still there when the Israelites stormed the city. (Josh. 6:22.)

Faith learns to be still when there is a shaking in our lives and simply to trust in the fact God knows what He is doing.

• TWENTY-EIGHT •
FAITH DEFINED

Hebrews 11:32-40

"And what shall I more say? for the time would fail me to tell of Gedeon, and of Barak, and of Samson, and of Jephthae..."

Judges 11:1-11

While a number of other individuals are mentioned in these verses, we will look at only one more person at this time. Jephthah was the son of a prostitute and his father Gilead also had a wife and other legitimate sons by her.

When grown, these other sons threw out Jephthah saying that he was not really one of the family and could not stay. So Jephthah, bitter in spirit and very disheartened became a member of a gang. Fighting became the way he expressed what he felt and became his way of life.

Faith forgives in order to do what God has purposed

Later, when the area in which he had grown up was experiencing war, the elders of the town came to Jephthah and asked him and his gang to help them. Jephthah's reply showed how bitter he was. "Why do you come to me when you hate me and have driven me out of my father's house? Why come now when you're in trouble?" (Jud. 11:7, Living Bible.) He did not plan to do them a favor now.

The wonderful thing about this story is that it speaks of forgiveness, and sometimes it is necessary to forgive in order to continue on in the purpose that God has for our lives. Hebrews later points this out. "Watch out that no bitterness takes root among you, for as it springs up it causes deep trouble, hurting many in their spiritual lives." (Heb. 12:15 Living Bible.) Jephthah did go back and help them fight, in fact he became their leader.

Faith does not always see the circumstances change favorably and often it is necessary to forgive in order to continue on the path that God sets out for us. Forgiving is not letting the other person or people off the hook for what they have done; it lets the person who forgives go free, free of bitterness and free from wanting revenge. In fact, it sets the person who forgives free to continue on in faith, confidently walking the pathway God intends for him or her to walk.

So what have we learned here?

We have learned that there has to be faith in order for us to be pleasing to God. The Living Bible puts it this way: "You can never please God without faith, without depending on him."

The whole world is based on faith; God created it that way. Things you never think about, like sitting on a chair requires faith to believe it will hold you as you do so.

There has to be faith that day will follow night and that the seasons will change according to their usual pattern.

Most of all there has to be faith in God, that He will be true to His Word in everything. That was the test Adam and Eve were faced with—to believe God meant what He said and that was what Satan disputed with them, and won.

We are required to believe God will do what He says, but in believing that, there is security and peace. Faith that is firmly rooted in the faithfulness of God is able to face anything this world offers. That's what it's all about.

UNDERSTANDING
The Epistle to the Hebrews

CONCLUSION
THE GOAL
Hebrews 12 and 13

• TWENTY-NINE •
THE PATTERN

Hebrews 12:1-13

"Wherefore seeing we also are compassed about with so great a cloud of witnesses, let us lay aside every weight, and the sin which doth so easily beset us, and let us run with patience the race that is set before us, looking unto Jesus the author and finisher of our faith..."

So what has been the purpose of this long discourse about people who lived and died with their faith intact? It shows God's goal for our lives.

While faith may begin by accepting Jesus Christ as our Savior and Lord, it mustn't stop there. God doesn't intend that we remain babies in our faith, or even toddlers; He wants mature sons — that's male and female sons!

So let's consider for a moment what is meant by sons. Jesus was the pattern son; that's what meant by calling Him the "author" of our faith. He set the mold. That's the goal.

Jesus, though He was born by the direct intervention of the Holy Spirit, was fully human. He had the same desires, temptations and lessons to learn as the rest of us. He was, in fact, the same as Adam who also was a human form with the Spirit of God breathed into him to give him life. (Adam is called a "son of God" in Luke 3:38.) So the potential is there in all humans, male and female alike.

A son, as God intended, was not intended to be a puppet. He made mankind to have freewill and to be able to make their own choices. But God wanted those choices always to be in line with His will. God's will is not a domineering force that wants everything His own way; God's will is the structure by which He runs the universe. When He made this world, everything was good and able to run according to a specific plan. But mankind messed it up and now God has called out people — born-again Christians — who can rise above all the imperfection and misuse, all the sin and unpleasantness, and become what God intended in the first place: sons. Sons are people of faith, who believe and walk, make their choices and plan their lives according to God's dictate. They love His way, choose His way and walk each step in the pathway He intended. That's the goal.

• THIRTY •
SPECIFIC INSTRUCTIONS
Hebrews 12:14 to 13:25

"Now the God of peace, that brought again from the dead our Lord Jesus, that great shepherd of the sheep, through the blood of the everlasting covenant, make you perfect in every good work to do his will, working in you that which is wellpleasing in his sight..."

Having written so many words about Jesus being the culmination of all that came before Him, and having pointed out that He is to be the pattern for our lives that will bring us to sonship (male and female) in Him, there has to follow some specific instructions. So the last two chapters of Hebrews simply state what to do and what not to do.

Beginning with several paragraphs concerning the need to recognize some things as God's correction in our lives, and to welcome this because it shows God is concerned and cares, the writer goes on to say "lift up the hands which hang down," or in other words: learn to get over it. Pity parties get a person nowhere and neither does bitterness. He addresses this in verse 15. Bitterness, if allowed in your heart, festers and grows like a disease until it controls all your outlook on life. It needs to be nipped in the bud right at the start.

"Follow peace with all men" is a principle to live by. It doesn't matter always to be proved right. Even if you are right and the other person wrong in their thinking, argument rarely benefits and may just make matters worse. Squash your pride and back down. You know what is right; God knows what is right and that's all that matters most of the time. If it's a question of sin, that's a little different.

The discourse about Esau is interesting, and brings to the front the desire to satisfy bodily craving rather than sticking with God's will and destiny. Or even allowing other things to creep in and take time from daily communion with Him.

Hospitality is mentioned and the need to remember to treat ministry people fairly and well, but the final words bring it all together when the writer gives the exhortation to "offer the sacrifice of praise to God continually, that is, the fruit of our lips giving thanks to his name" and not to forget to "communicate" with Him, since God is the key to our lives.

In the
WILDERNESS
God's Lessons for
Changing Ordinary People
into His People

by Lyn Gitchel

A SERIES OF BIBLE STUDIES

In the letter to the Corinthians, Paul points out that the events that happened during the time the Israelites were in the wilderness were not just recorded as history. They were recorded for us to learn by those same lessons, he says.

In this series of Bible studies, Lyn Gitchel shows how the lessons God taught them are as relevant for Christians today.

Divided also into four sections suitable for group study.

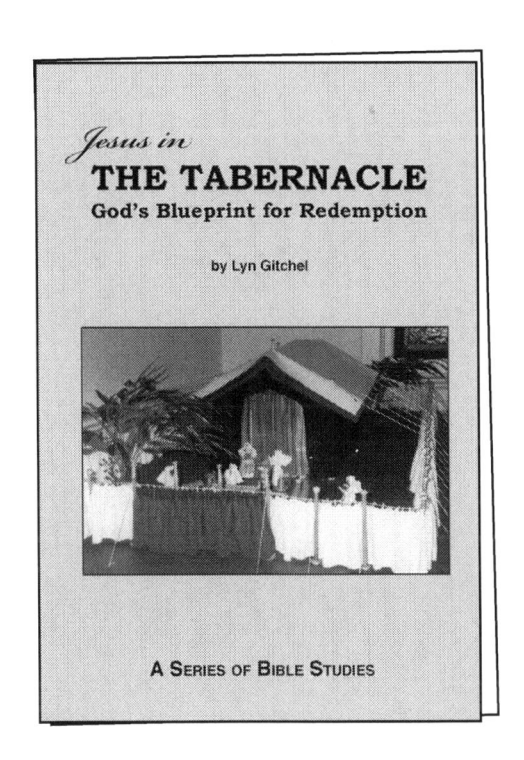

A series of Bible Studies showing how, in the days before there were any written scriptures, God painted a picture of redemption. Written into the symbolism of the place of worship that God planned for the Israelites while in the wilderness, is the personality of Jesus, who he was, his sacrifice on the cross and details of the redemption that he accomplished for mankind.

lyngitchel@gmail.com

Made in the USA
Columbia, SC
06 April 2022